Anglican
Curate

Ruth Nason

Photographs by Chris Fairclough

W
FRANKLIN WATTS
LONDON·SYDNEY

First published in 2001 by
Franklin Watts
96 Leonard Street
London EC2A 4XD

Franklin Watts Australia
56 O'Riordan Street
Alexandria
NSW 2015

ISBN 0 7496 4064 2

Dewey Decimal Classification Number 283

A CIP catalogue record for this book is
available from the British Library

Design: Carole Binding

Reading Consultant: Lesley Clark, Reading
and Language Information Centre, University
of Reading

The Author and Publishers thank
the Revd Canon Anthony Hulbert,
Revd Nicola Lenthall and all the people at
All Saints, Leighton Buzzard, for their help in
preparing this book.

Printed in Malaysia

Contents

Hello!

I'm Nicola.
I am the curate
of an Anglican
church called
All Saints.

I am also a priest in the church. This means that I can lead important ceremonies.

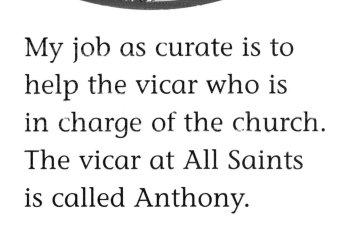

My job as curate is to help the vicar who is in charge of the church. The vicar at All Saints is called Anthony.

Our church

All Saints church is 700 years old. At the moment the tower is being repaired and so there is plastic and scaffolding around it.

All Saints is the main church for everyone who lives in the surrounding area. This area is called the parish.

A church is a building. But we also say that all the people who come to All Saints make up our church.

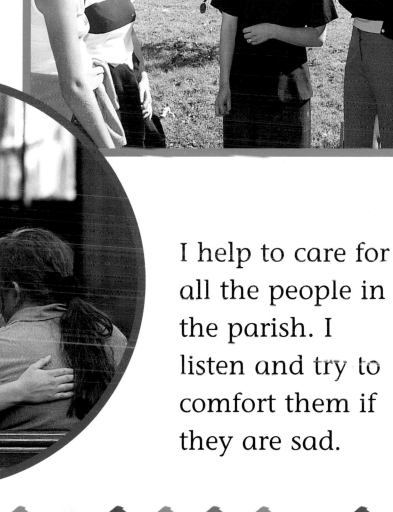

I help to care for all the people in the parish. I listen and try to comfort them if they are sad.

Services

A service is a time when people can come to church to pray and worship God. There are services every day. Most people come to one of the Sunday services.

Leading services is part of my job as curate.

At many services we sing hymns and prayers. Our organist usually plays the music and the choir leads the singing.

We also have a music group. It plays at family services.

11

Sermons

In some services I go up into the pulpit to give a talk called a sermon.

In my sermons, I talk about what we can learn from the Bible. Often, I talk about Jesus.

Jesus lived 2,000 years ago. He told people about God's love. But then he was put to death on a cross.

Christians believe that God sent Jesus into the world, to show people how God wanted them to be. They believe that, after he died, Jesus came alive again and went to live for ever with God, in heaven. They believe that Jesus is God's son.

Bread and wine

Jesus told his followers to share bread
and wine, as a way of remembering
him. This is why Anglicans have a
ceremony called the Eucharist,
when we share bread and wine.
Everything we use for the
ceremony is very special.

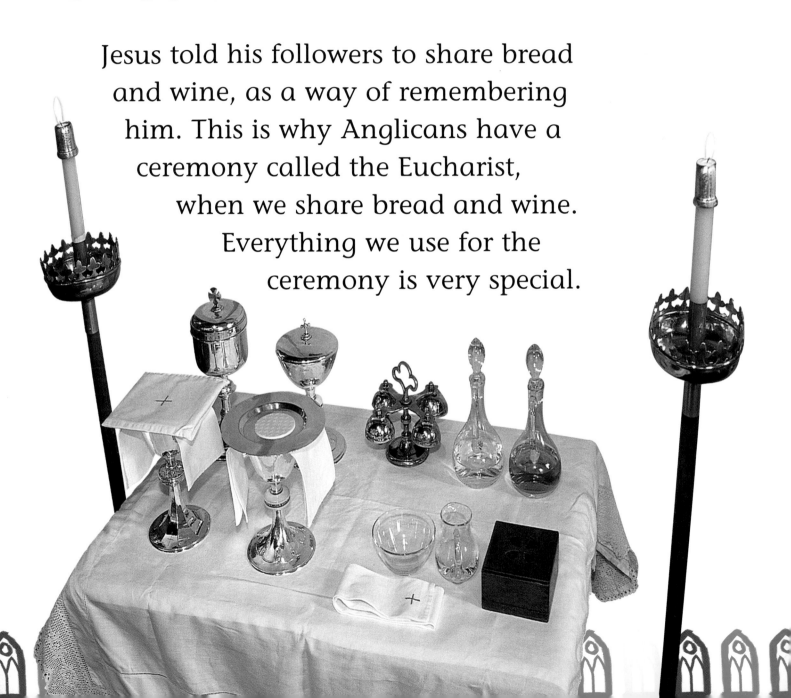

A server helps me set everything out on the altar. It is like laying a table. Then he washes my hands.

Later the server helps me to give people the special bread and a sip of wine.

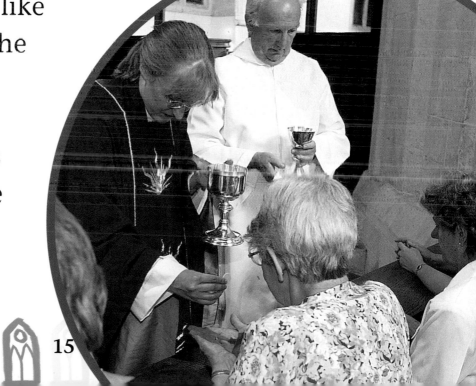

15

Baptism

Baptism is a ceremony for someone starting to be a Christian. Many parents want their new baby to be baptised. In the ceremony, they promise to bring their child up as a Christian. I pour water on the baby's head.

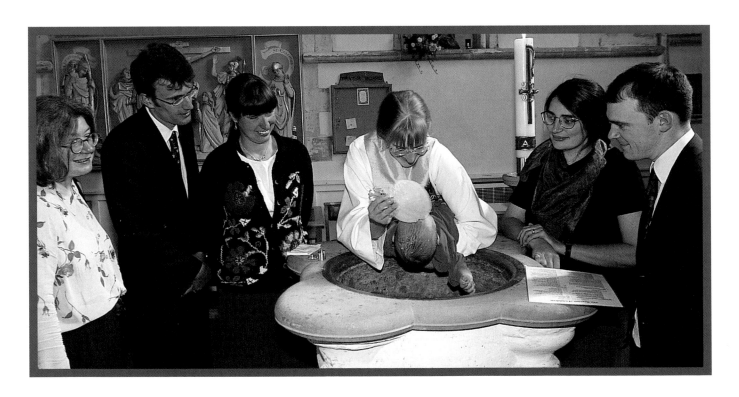

The church gives the family a candle, to remind them of the baptism.

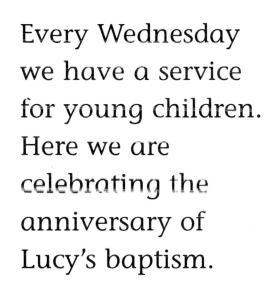

Every Wednesday we have a service for young children. Here we are celebrating the anniversary of Lucy's baptism.

Marriage

Many couples want to be married at All Saints. First the church must check that no one knows any reason why a couple can't be married. So their names are read out at three Sunday services. This is called reading the banns.

Then I sign a certificate to say that the banns have been read. Now the marriage can go ahead.

At the marriage service, the couple promise to stay together and look after each other for ever. They give each other rings.

Afterwards, the couple sign the marriage register. I sign it too, to say that I have married them.

At home

I live with my husband Adrian. We enjoy doing things together, like cycling and playing music.

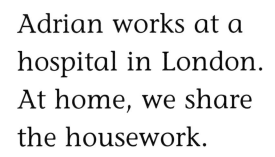

Adrian works at a hospital in London. At home, we share the housework.

My study

We live in a house which belongs to
the church. My study is the room
where I plan services. I read, pray,
think and write notes for my sermons.

Clothes

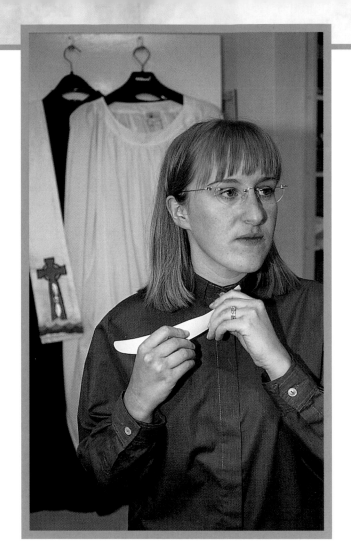

When I go out, I wear a clerical collar. The collar slots into my shirt.

The gowns I wear for services hang on my study door. I wear the white surplice on top of the black cassock.

I also wear a stole for all services.
A stole is rather like a scarf.

I wear one of these beautiful chasubles when I lead the Eucharist.

For leading a funeral service (a service for someone who has died), I wear a purple stole.

A curate's day

I have many things to do each day and every day is different. Here are some examples from just one day.

To start the day, I say prayers in my study.

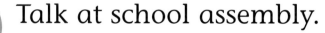

Talk at school assembly.

Join in staff meeting.

Show school group around church.

Attend the lunchtime Eucharist.

25

Eat lunch in the church coffee shop.

Lead the children's service.

Meet with church gardener.

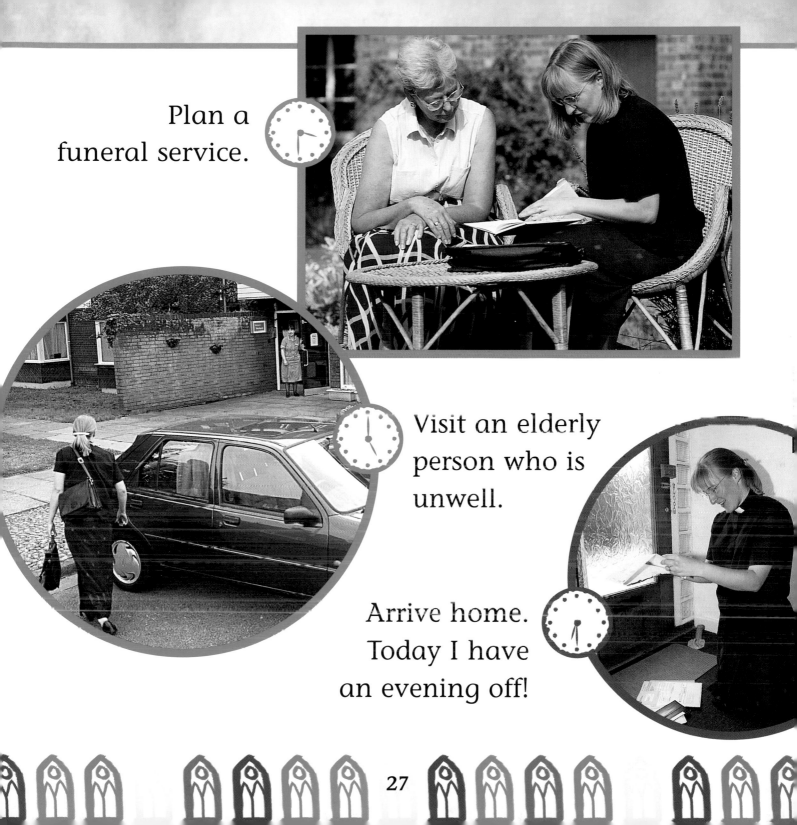

Plan a
funeral service.

Visit an elderly
person who is
unwell.

Arrive home.
Today I have
an evening off!

Glossary

altar

The table used for the Eucharist.

Anglican

Belonging to the Anglican Church. The Anglican Church is one part of the Christian Church, which means all Christians all over the world.

Bible

The Christian holy book.

ceremony

A set of actions, always done in the same way and with the same words. The actions and words have a special meaning for the people taking part.

Christians

People who follow the teachings of Jesus.

church

A building where Christians meet to worship God. Also, all the people who worship there together are called the church.

clergy

All the people, like curates and vicars, who are church ministers.

clerical

To do with the clergy.

cross

The main symbol of Christianity.

curate

An Anglican church minister who assists (helps) a vicar.

Eucharist

An important ceremony for Anglicans.

hymn

A song to worship God.

organist

Someone who plays the organ, a musical instrument found in many churches.

parish

An area which has its own Anglican church. The whole country is divided into parishes.

priest

A church minister who has been given the special task of leading important ceremonies.

pulpit

A kind of raised box in which a church minister stands to preach.

server

Someone who has the task of helping the priest at the Eucharist.

vicar

An Anglican church minister who is in charge of a parish and its church.

Index